Midnight Bakery

Written by Sharon Parsons

Contents		Page
Chapter 1.	*Before Baking Begins*	4
Chapter 2.	*The Baking Race*	8
Feature:	*Easy Yeast Experiments*	10
Chapter 3.	*The Race Continues*	18
Chapter 4.	*Help Is On The Way*	25
Index And Bookweb Links		32
Glossary		Inside Back Cover

Chapter Snapshots

1. Before Baking Begins Page 4
While most people are asleep, work is just starting for our three bakers, Mick, Trevor, and Brenna.

2. The Baking Race Page 8
With hundreds of loaves, buns, rolls, and pizza crusts to bake, our bakers need a lot of dough!

3. The Race Continues Page 18
The ovens are full and the delicious smell of hot bread fills the bakery!

4. Help Is On The Way Page 25
The last of the bakery products are shaped and baked; and by the time most people are waking up, our bakers have been working for hours, preparing for the first customers.

"Bakers are fast, accurate

A Bakery Layout

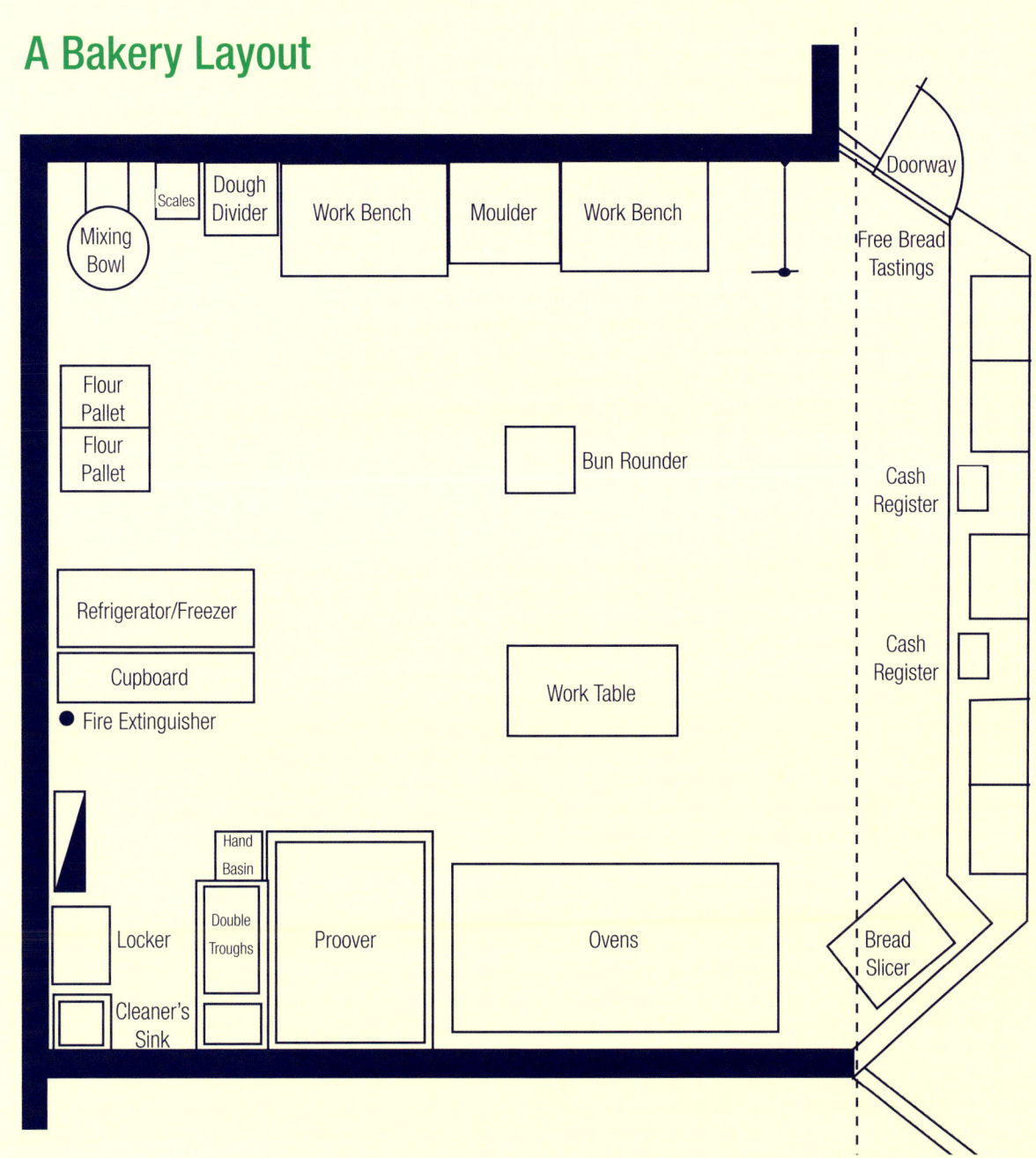

and organized ..."

1. Before Baking Begins

Wake-Up Call!

It's a freezing winter's night and Mick, a baker, sleeps soundly. Suddenly, his alarm clock buzzes loudly and shocks him awake. Only an hour to go before midnight, when he starts his job at the bakery.

The bakery at night.

Trevor, another baker, who works with Mick, starts at 12:20 that morning.

Trevor and Mick make sure their hands are clean.

At 3:50 A.M., Mick and Trevor are joined by a third baker, Brenna. She was allowed to sleep in today, as she started work at 12:30 last night.

What do each of these bakers have in common? They enjoy early morning work and they are fit, strong, and organized. Their minds are sharp as they calculate and organize the correct amounts of ingredients from their recipe books at lightning speed! They bake hundreds of different bakery products every day.

Brenna arrives for work at 3:50 A.M.

Hygiene And Safety

As part of their training, bakers learn that food hygiene and workplace safety are as important as baking quality products.

Every machine has built-in safety features, but the bakers must still learn how to operate them safely to prevent accidents.

The mixing bowl.

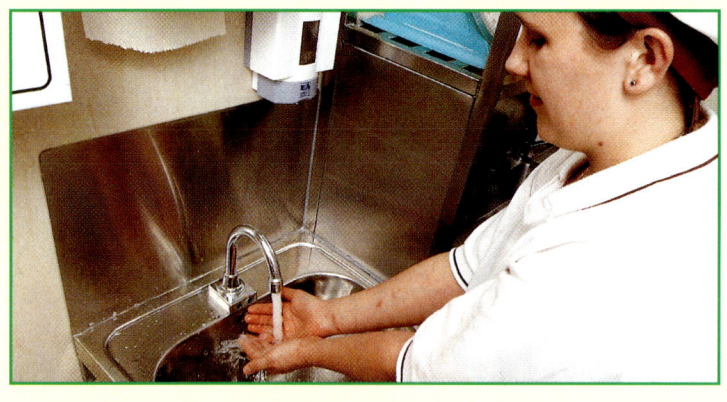

Brenna makes sure that her hands are clean.

Bakers wear a clean uniform that includes a hat to cover their hair, an apron, and non-slip safety shoes.

Before bakers start performing their work, they must wash their hands with an anti-bacterial solution to kill any germs. If bakers use the toilet, touch any part of their faces, or handle money, they must stop and wash their hands again.

The bakers stop for a drink.

Inside a bakery, it is hotter than a summer's day, so bakers must drink plenty of water or juice to prevent dehydration. For safety, they can drink only from plastic containers. The bakers take turns having drink breaks, but only when someone has a few seconds to spare!

As often as they can, the bakers sweep the floor, which can become slippery when seeds and flour fall off the work benches.

All ingredients and bakery products are prepared and handled in hygienic conditions. The benches are made of shiny stainless steel, and the floor is covered with a non-slip safety surface.

Trevor and Mick clean the floor.

2. The Baking Race

Mick arrives at 12:10 A.M. to turn on the oven and the proover because it takes them half an hour to heat up to the right temperature.

Next, he quickly gets ready to make 165 pounds of white dough, so that approximately 500 bakery products, such as loaves, rolls, and mini-pizzas, can be prepared in time for the first customers!

A Fast And Safe Baking Team

Watching bakers at work, especially in the first two hours of their day, is like being a spectator at a race. The bakers can't stop until their baking requirements are complete!

Always thinking about safety, bakers are fast, accurate, and organized, so that they can bake the best-quality bread on time. They work as a team, helping each other out so they do not waste precious seconds.

Mick weighs the salt for the dough mixture.

Mick weighs the dry ingredients, such as flour, salt, and improver, and measures the liquids, such as water and oil. Then he is ready to add them to the huge mixing bowl.

Making The Dough

Step 1

Mick adds the water first.

Step 2

Oil is poured from the measuring jug.

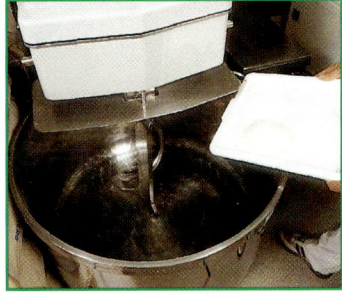

Step 3

The salt and the improver are added.

Step 4

In goes the baker's flour.

Step 5

Yeast is the last ingredient to be added.

Step 6

Mick programs the electric mixer's speed. After four minutes, the mixer automatically changes to a faster speed for 14 minutes so that the ingredients are combined into high-quality dough.

Easy Yeast Experiments

Experience how powerful baker's yeast can be by trying these experiments for yourself.

A Baker's Experiment

Sometimes bakers forget if they have added yeast to the dough mixture. They check by dropping a lump of dough into a glass of water.

Try it for yourself! What happens when you drop one lump of dough with yeast and one lump without yeast into a glass of water? Which dough rises to the top of the glass?

Dough Stretches And Bounces!
Dough containing gluten stretches like bubblegum! When you roll it into the shape of a ball, it can even bounce!

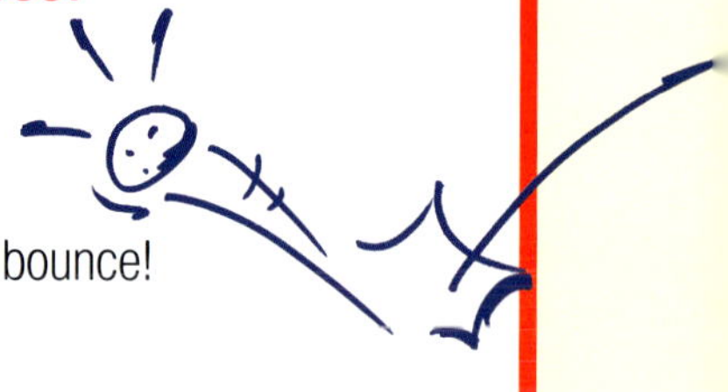

A Runny Experiment

Place a teaspoon of baker's yeast on top of three teaspoons of salt on a flat surface. After three minutes, the yeast will gradually change from a solid substance to a liquid.

A Frothy Experiment

Mix two teaspoons of sugar and two teaspoons of fresh yeast with a little warm water. After 10 minutes, you will see some bubbles. After 40 minutes, the surface of the mixture will be frothy. The frothy bubbles are the gas, carbon dioxide, that the yeast makes when it feeds on the sugar.

Yeast

Yeast is a type of fungus. It needs food, water, and warmth to grow. In the bread-making process, yeast is fed salt, flour, and water. As it grows, it produces bubbles of gas that cause the dough to rise.

   By placing dough in the warm proover, the yeast works even better to make the dough become higher and lighter! It can't rise forever, though. Once the yeast has "eaten" all the food it can in the dough, it collapses. The bakers must start to bake the dough before that happens!

Trevor arrives at 12:20 A.M. to the sound of the mixer whirring. He knows that he must quickly put on his uniform and wash his hands. Mick has already turned on the radio to their favorite station.

The 165 pounds of dough that Mick prepared earlier will be ready in 10 minutes!

Did You Know?
The busiest day of the year at a bakery is the Thursday before Good Friday, when thousands of hot-cross buns are sold.

It's Saturday, the bakery's busiest day of the week, so the bakers know they will have to double the usual amount of white dough and whole wheat dough: 1,100 pounds! That's a lot of dough when you know that one loaf of bread starts out as 28 ounces of dough and one small dinner roll starts out as 1.4 ounces of dough.

First, the bakers must prepare hundreds of bakery products, from the dough they have mixed, in the next 45 minutes!

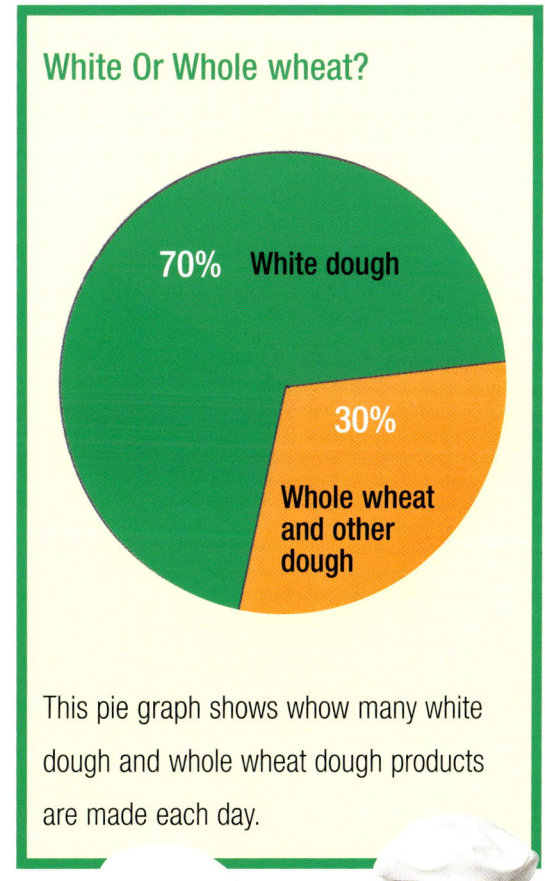

White Or Whole wheat?

70% White dough

30% Whole wheat and other dough

This pie graph shows whow many white dough and whole wheat dough products are made each day.

Mick and Trevor discuss today's production schedule. It lists how many of each bakery product they need to bake this morning.

Bakery Recipes

This morning, Trevor and Mick will make 60 different recipes. But when they started working at the bakery, they had to learn how to make about 300 different recipes!

Bakers have memorized most of their recipes, but they always check the recipe books, even when they are busy.

At-Home Recipes

Have some fun and make some sandwich and roll recipes of your own!

A Sweet Sandwich Recipe

Rumble In The Jungle
Ingredients
Banana

Cinnamon

Cream cheese

Honey

Dried fruit

Method
Combine ingredients and make as a toasted sandwich.

Savory Lunch Recipes

Chicky Babe

Ingredients
Chicken
Pesto
Mayonnaise
Alfalfa sprouts

Method
Combine ingredients and make on a sesame seed shell roll.

Chook-A-Doodle-Do

Ingredients
Hard-boiled egg
Celery
Lettuce
Mayonnaise

Method
Combine ingredients and make as a normal sandwich.

Green Eggs And Ham

Ingredients
Fried egg
Ham
Spinach

Method
Combine ingredients and make as a toasted sandwich.

Worms'n'All

Ingredients
Spaghetti
Swiss cheese

Method
Combine ingredients and make as a toasted sandwich.

From The Bowl To The Resting Racks

Step 1
It's 12:40 A.M. The dough has been mixed and has rested for 10 minutes in the mixing bowl at the right temperature.

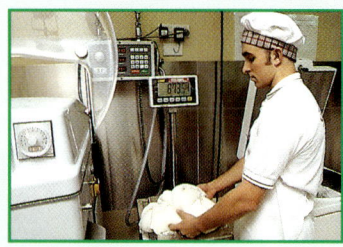

Step 2
Huge chunks of dough are cut from the bowl and weighed on the electronic scales.

Step 3
When Trevor reads the correct weight, he places the dough onto the dough divider's floured surface.

Step 4
The dough divider, often called the "magic machine," can divide a lump of dough into 20 equal portions within three seconds!

Step 5
Each portion of the dough is ready to be placed on the resting rack.

Step 6
The dough will rest for about half an hour before the bakers can start preparing bakery products.

A Baker's Quote:
"All work and no rest makes dough a dull boy!"

In the first 45 minutes, Mick and Trevor are so busy they rarely talk about what each is doing—they just know what each other's jobs are. They like working together because they enjoy working quickly.

"It's easier to work fast than to slow down," they say enthusiastically.

Resting

Resting the dough for 10 minutes in the mixing bowl and for at least half an hour on the resting racks enhances the flavor of the bread. If the dough doesn't rest, it will be too tight and difficult to work with.

Bakers call it "resting" because the dough has just been mixed on a fast speed—they liken it to people resting after running a race.

Trevor updates the production schedule with details of all the bakery products that have been prepared in the first 45 minutes.

3. The Race Continues

Why Bakers Work So Fast

To work fast and efficiently, bakers must be organized! They always clean up after themselves and put things back in the right place so that they can find them quickly. Three reasons why they must work quickly are:

1. The dough contains yeast so it is growing. If the dough rests for too long, it loses its strength and moisture and may collapse.

2. The bakers must coordinate the timing of the bakery products at every stage of the bread-making process. To do this, they must use their equipment quickly and effectively.

3. A small selection of bakery products should be ready for customers at 3:30 A.M. but a full range must be ready by 6:00 A.M.

From The Resting Racks To The Proover

After the dough has rested for half an hour, each baker works extra quickly to prepare and shape the portions of dough into a wide range of bakery products.

Mick and Trevor make mini-pizzas.

By 1:30 A.M., 500 different products have been prepared and shaped. They rest in the proover for half an hour before they are baked.

Twenty Buns In Two Minutes!

1. Thirty seconds
Flattening the dough.

2. Thirty seconds
Rolling the dough.

3. Thirty-five seconds
Hand-rolling the dough.

4. Twenty seconds
Cutting the poppy seed buns.

5. Five seconds
Placing the buns into the proover.

The Proover

Inside the proover, which looks like a huge cabinet, is a carefully controlled warm and humid environment. The warmth helps the yeast in the dough to grow, and the humidity prevents the dough from drying out.

The dough remains inside the proover for about 30 to 40 minutes. That's long enough for the dough to rise, but not to grow too large and spill over the sides of the tins and trays!

1:32 A.M.

After Trevor and Mick review the production schedule and drink some water, they start making the scones.

Fifteen pounds of scone mixture ends up as 180 scones in four minutes! The most popular scones are date scones. Mick is kneading the scone mixture that Trevor made earlier. He is pleased with its texture, so he says, "Nice scones, Trev!"

"Nice scones, Trev!"

2:05 A.M.

After 30 to 40 minutes in the proover, the trays of dough are removed. The dough for the loaves, buns, and bread sticks has doubled in size.

Dough that has just come out of the proover.

Before Trevor places the trays in the oven, he is careful to follow the golden rule—never drop or bump them hard. If the baker accidentally does this, the gas that has caused the dough to rise will escape, and the bread will not rise to the right height in the oven.

Once the ovens are full, Trevor helps Mick with the mini-pizzas and other savory products.

2:25 A.M.

The oven timers are buzzing! The first batch of bakery products has finished baking. Trevor already knew they were ready, because he could smell the fabulous aroma of hot bread!

Trevor wears special oven mitts to protect his hands from burns as he removes tins and trays.

Usually it takes 25 to 27 minutes to bake normal-sized white loaves and 12 to 18 minutes to bake rolls.

When Is A Loaf Of Bread Baked?

When the baker carefully tips the baked loaves of bread out of the tins onto cooling trays, he taps one loaf on the bottom. If it makes a deep, hollow sound, he is certain that they are all baked perfectly.

It's Breakfast Time!

There's a feeling of excitement as both bakers decide which of the warm crusty rolls to eat for breakfast. They decide to have cheese and bacon rolls topped with their own barbecue sauce.

"Great rolls, Mick," says Trevor.

The first batch of bakery products has been unloaded from the ovens, so it's now breakfast time!

Which Bakery Products Are Popular With Kids?
White dinner rolls, ham and cheese pockets, chocolate éclairs and mini-pizzas. Yum!

3:30 A.M.

Mick has just finished serving a regular customer, a musician on his way home from work. He bought croissants and a loaf of hot bread, fresh out of the oven.

Now, the pace in the bakery slows down, if just a little!

> **A Baker's Checklist At 3:30 A.M.**
> ✓ Selection of bakery products ready for customers to buy.
> ✓ Second batch of dough is mixing in the bowl.
> ✓ Resting racks are full.
> ✓ Proover is full.
> ✓ Ovens are full.

Mick checks that there are enough chopped ingredients, such as onions and mushrooms, in the fridge. They don't want to run out when they are busily making such savory products as mini-pizzas.

4. Help Is On The Way

Brenna, The Third Baker, Arrives!

Before Brenna can check the second batch of dough in the mixing bowl, she must complete three important health and safety requirements.

Step 1
Brenna puts on her clean apron.

Step 2
She tucks her hair under the hat.

Step 3
Brenna washes her hands with anti-bacterial soap.

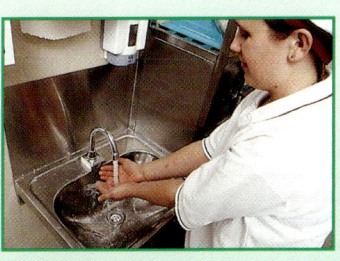

Trevor Works With The Ovens

Now that Brenna has started work, Trevor can spend all his time watching the ovens and calling out what he needs and when he needs it.

Who Really Controls The Bakery?

Although every baker helps the others with different jobs, it is the baker operating the ovens who really controls the bakery production. The timing is critical. The baker organizes the tins and trays on the decks so that each oven will not be empty for too long. The decks move in a circular motion so that the bakery products bake evenly.

Brenna Works With Mick

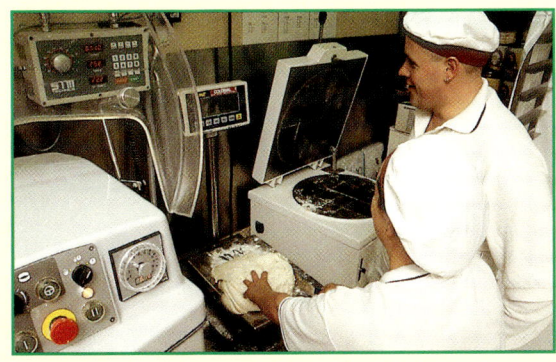

Brenna places the dough onto the electronic scales.

Brenna cuts large chunks of dough out of the mixing bowl.

Once the dough weighs 35 pounds, Mick places it onto the dough divider's floured surface. The bakers like using a special "number" code that only they can understand!

Mick, we need four, five, three, two and one!

Okay, I'll make four white blocks, five small white flour loaves, three tin viennas, make two cuts of dough for shell and knot rolls, and one cut for dinner rolls.

Brenna Works Alone

By 4:30 A.M., Brenna reviews the production schedule to find out the remaining bakery requirements. She starts molding dough into different bakery products.

Brenna proudly calls herself the "Vienna Queen." She hand-molds the dough for Vienna loaves into perfect shapes.

The Bun Rounder

When students visit the bakery, they often comment that the bun rounder machine looks like the R2D2 character in the movie *Star Wars*.

Brenna operates the bun-rounder machine.

Seconds later, thirty perfectly shaped rolls are formed!

Brenna Makes Bread Sticks

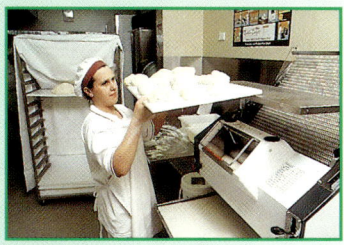

Step 1
Brenna lifts a tray of dough pieces to the molder machine.

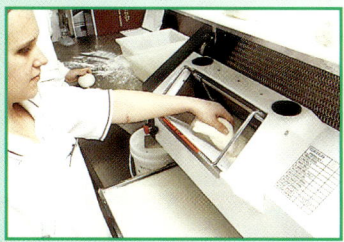

Step 2
She carefully places a portion of dough in the roller section.

Step 3
Brenna lifts the bread stick shape from the bottom tray.

Step 4
She coats the bread stick dough with poppy seeds.

Step 5
Sesame and poppy seed bread sticks are baked in the same wavy-shaped tray.

Mick Dances Alone!

Mick is still busy, but not as frantic as he was earlier on. So what does he do when he hears his favorite song on the radio? He starts singing and dancing in front of the mixing bowl!

Bakers work extremely hard, so they fit in some fun whenever they can!

Customer Service

Erin, a bakery assistant, arrives at 5:45 A.M. to serve customers. During the morning, people buy a range of bakery products but they mostly buy savory and fruit products and croissants. One of the busiest times in a bakery is between 7:00 A.M. and 8:00 A.M. when many people buy bakery products for breakfast and lunch.

Slicing Bread: Health And Safety

To help customers, Erin always asks if they would like toast- or sandwich-sliced bread.

For hygiene reasons, Erin never touches the bread. She uses small paper sheets and a plastic bag. For safety reasons, she keeps her fingers clear of the cutting blades.

Customers choose some bakery products to add to their school lunches. Erin provides friendly customer service.

The End Of A Long Day!

Baking continues throughout the day so that customers always have freshly baked products to buy. The three bakers are joined by another baker and an apprentice baker. By noon, Mick, Trevor, and Brenna can go home! More serving staff arrive at different times to work during the day.

The Bread Machine

For people who don't have a bakery close by, a bread-making machine comes in handy. All you need to do is place all the ingredients into the machine's bowl, push a few buttons and a loaf of bread is finished in two to four hours.

Trevor and Mick pack up before they leave for the day.

By 8:00 P.M., the bakery has been open for business for 20 hours! There are not many products left. Someone has taken the unsold products to a homeless shelter—the shelves, racks and cabinets are empty once more!

Index

bread
- loaves 8, 13, 21, 22, 24, 27, 28
- rolls 8, 13, 22, 23, 27
- scrolls 19
- sticks 21, 29

bread machine 31
bun rounder 28
croissants 23, 24, 30
customers 8, 18, 24, 30, 31
dehydration 7
dough 8, 9, 10, 11, 12, 13, 16, 17, 18, 19, 21, 27, 28
germs 6
hot-cross buns 12
hygiene 6, 7, 12, 25, 30
ingredients 9
mixer, electric 9
oven 8, 21, 22, 23, 26
pizza 8, 24
production schedule 13, 17, 20, 24, 28
proover 8, 19, 21
recipes 14, 15
safety 6, 7, 8, 22, 25, 30
sandwiches 14, 15
scones 20
uniform 6
yeast 9, 10, 11, 18, 19

Bookweb Links

More Bookweb books
about baking, hygiene and safety.

The Great Egg Problem—Fiction
Ugly Pugsy—Fiction
Germ Warfare—Nonfiction
Disaster Plan—Nonfiction

Key To Bookweb Fact Boxes
- ☐ Arts
- ☐ Health
- ☐ Science
- ☐ Social Studies
- ☐ Technology